GLAD YOU'RE
BACK

GLAD YOU'RE
BACK

G. MICHAEL GOWER

TATE PUBLISHING
AND ENTERPRISES, LLC

Published by Tate Publishing & Enterprises, LLC
127 E. Trade Center Terrace | Mustang, Oklahoma 73064 USA
1.888.361.9473 | www.tatepublishing.com

Tate Publishing is committed to excellence in the publishing industry. The company reflects the philosophy established by the founders, based on Psalm 68:11,
"The Lord gave the word and great was the company of those who published it."

Book design copyright © 2014 by Tate Publishing, LLC. All rights reserved.
Cover design by Nikolai Purpura

Published in the United States of America

ISBN: 978-1-63185-672-3
1. Biography & Autobiography / Military
2. History / Military / Vietnam War
14.06.18

DEDICATION

This book is dedicated to all of the Americans and our Allies who served in the Vietnam War. To the brave P.O.W.'s. To those who returned home, and to the memory of those who didn't. To those who are still listed as Missing In Action - may we someday have the opportunity to welcome them home.

To the memory of my brother Mark, who died in a motorcycle accident only thirty days prior to being honorably discharged from active duty in the U.S. Navy.

And to Gay - my hero

CHAPTERS

Leaving for 'Nam

Going...

going...

gone.

CHAPTER ONE

ORDERS FOR 'NAM

After completing Basic Combat Training, which began for me in January, 1969, I was more than ready to bid farewell to Fort Leonard Wood, Missouri (We called it Fort "Lost-In-The-Woods", because we were certain that only God and the U.S. Army knew for certain where this place was located). However, I was given no leave after Basic, and was even held over for two weeks, until my A.I.T. (Advanced Individual Training) class started. I was rather nervous during this time, not knowing what to expect. We *all* felt that we could whip the known world with one hand tied behind us, but that's how we were *supposed* to feel. We had been trained to think that way.

A.I.T. was a different ball game, though. Taking on the world in mortal combat was one thing, but learning avionics was another challenge altogether. My M.O.S.(Military Occupation

Specialty) was 35M20 - Avionics Navigation Equipment Repair. I really had no idea exactly what I would be learning or doing, but I knew that if it was more complicated than 9th grade algebra, it wouldn't be easy. For this training, I was finally sent to Fort Gordon, Georgia, where I spent eighteen weeks learning to troubleshoot and repair aircraft electronic navigation equipment. Localizer, V.O.R., glideslope, and A.D.F. were among the electronic systems that we were expected to learn in what we felt was a very short time. We did the job, though, and were looking forward to graduation - and leave time! However, we were more than a bit anxious about where our next duty station would be.

Fort Gordon wasn't a bad place to be, as Army posts go, though both the temperature and the humidity got higher as the summer of 1969 progressed. The U. S. Army Signal School operated in shifts, and I was on the night shift. We marched to the classrooms at 3:00 P.M., and marched back to the barracks at midnight.

I remember the week that Apollo 11 was launched, a few guys pooled their money and rented a small black and white T.V. from a rental store on post, so that we could watch the event live, up in our barracks room. There was a color set in the Day Room, but most everything on it was green or orange, depending on the weather conditions (nope, no cable yet). When the Lunar Lander was making its' approach to the moon's surface, it was so quiet in that room that you could almost *literally* hear a pin drop - on the cement and tile floor! I don't know how long we held our breath, but when we heard, "Tranquility Base here. The Eagle has landed", pandemonium broke out! We were so happy and proud, we were jumping on our bunks, yelling, whistling - all that stuff. The same thing happened again when Neil Armstrong made that "one small step" on the lunar surface. We were nearly bouncing off the walls! For a few brief moments that night, it didn't seem to matter what was to come after Signal School. If we *thought* that we were invincible after Basic, we *knew* we were now. Americans had landed on the moon! We were Americans too, and we felt that we could do ANYTHING!

About three weeks prior to our scheduled graduation, I was called into the School Commander's office, along with two other guys. We were informed that our grades had been higher than any others recorded in the last two years, and upon graduation, we would likely be promoted from Private E2 to SP4(Specialist 4th Class - E4), and train to be instructors at the school. Three of the instructors were due to rotate out soon, and we would be there replacements. Of course, this scenario all depended on our scores maintaining their present high level (and they did). This was wonderful news to us. Stateside duty during a war. How lucky could we get?!

Finally, it was time for graduation. After the ceremony, we got our promotion orders, and our next assignments. Our entire class was promoted to Private First Class (E3), and we *all* got orders sending us to Vietnam. Not a really good day. We were to receive fifteen days leave before departing for 'Nam, but only after we were held over at Fort Gordon for two weeks of "jungle training". Also, since most of us had qualified with the M-14 rifle in Basic, we all had to be re-qualified - this time, with the M-16. It was the Army's new weapon-of-choice in Vietnam. It was supposed to be America's answer to the AK-47 that the North Vietnamese and Viet Cong were using. The M-16 was lighter and shorter than the M-14, and it really packed a punch, but my favorite was still the M-14. I could hit *anything* with it - even at 350 meters. I also thought that with the right scope, it might make a good deer rifle.

At last, we finished our jungle training, and got ready to head for home on leave. Fifteen days didn't give us a lot of time at home before leaving for a minimum one-year tour in Vietnam. We all felt that we should have received at least thirty days leave before heading into a combat zone! We said our good-byes and promised to keep in touch somehow, but keeping track of each other wasn't realistic, and I think that deep down we all knew it. Mostly, we knew that we only had fifteen days to make some really big decisions - decisions that could very well change our lives forever.

CHAPTER TWO

SCARED?

Fear is an unpredictable thing. It can make you run faster than you've ever run, jump higher than you've ever jumped, and lift things that one person should never be able to lift alone. It can make your body become as limp as a wet noodle, or freeze you in your tracks - as solid and immovable as a stone statue. It can also make you do other things that you never in your life thought you were capable of doing.

I guess the lesser types of fear are just called anxiety. I think that was what I was feeling as I traveled back to Kansas for my hard-earned fifteen day leave. Although I was eager to return home, and excited about seeing family and friends again, I was sobered by the thought that during this short fifteen days, my fiancee, Gay, and I would have to make at least one major decision. It would not be easy for either of us.

We had originally planned to be married when I returned on leave after Basic, but since I got no leave at that time, we decided to be wed after Signal School - depending on where my next duty station would be. The prospect of my being assigned to the Signal School as an instructor was exciting news for us, but those hopes evaporated as soon as I received my reassignment orders.

The orders sending me to South Vietnam really put us in a quandary. Do we get married before I leave for 'Nam, or wait until after I returned? All the while, I think we both knew that there was always the possibility that I might not return - at least, not alive. I wasn't as concerned about that as much as Gay was, though. I was more afraid that I would be badly wounded or disfigured in a way that would make me undesirable to the young woman that I loved. I was well aware of the possibilities, and I had enlisted voluntarily, so I knew what the risks were from the beginning. Gay, however, was not blessed with my insight into the situation. I was the one who would have to play the "tough guy". After all, I was the one who could "whip the world…..etc.", right? Sure. Right.

I had turned twenty years old in June, 1969, and Gay was just shy of nineteen. This was a girl that I had met when we were both in Jr. High, and we wanted *so much* to be husband and wife. However, I didn't want her to be faced with the prospect of becoming a teenage widow, even though I fully expected to return to her alive and well. So , hard as it was, we decided to wait until I got back from 'Nam to get married.

I'm sure that she was a bit scared, or at least apprehensive, about marrying me even if I did return from the war. It is said that war changes people, you know. I was a bit scared about that, too. I could plug a pop-up target at 350 meters - no sweat. But Rifle Range targets aren't *people*, and they never shoot back. I was scared about the unknown factors involved in going to war - the things that the Army *didn't* prepare me for. I was afraid that the Vietnam war might turn me into

9

someone that I really didn't want to be - or someone that Gay might decide she couldn't be married to. That would have been devastating for us both, I think.

Shortly before my leave was over, I was contacted by Mrs. Shirley Dyck, a former teacher from Maize High School. I had written to Mrs. Dyck a couple of times while I was In Basic, and at least once during Signal School. I had gone into one of the " 4 photos for 25 cents" booths, and sent her some pictures of me and my nearly-bald head. I thought that she might get a laugh or two out of them. While I was home on leave, she called and invited Gay and me out for dinner. We met Mrs. Dyck and her husband, Harry, at a very nice Chinese restaurant in Wichita. We had a great time laughing and joking about past times at Maize High. Mrs. Dyck caught me up on the happenings at M.H.S. since I had graduated, and she and Harry asked me all kinds of questions about the Army, and my training, and all that. She also informed me that it would be all right for me to call her "Shirley", since we were no longer teacher and student. However, I just couldn't bring myself to do that. I told her that I respected her so much (and still do) that I was certain that God would strike me with a lightning bolt if I ever addressed her by anything other than "Mrs. Dyck". We all laughed about that, and after enjoying a fine meal and a fun visit, our evening came to an end. When we parted company in the parking lot of the restaurant, Mrs. Dyck gave me a hug, and told me to "Be careful over there in Vietnam". Unlike today, hugs were not given out very freely in those days, so that hug meant a great deal to me. Also, to be invited to dinner by a former teacher was something that I considered to be a great honor. Harry is gone now, but I still stay in contact with Mrs. Dyck, and I still think that she is a very great lady.

Finally, my leave came to an end, and I reluctantly boarded a plane for Oakland, California, where I would undergo overseas processing. For a twenty-year-old kid from Maize, Kansas, America, it was sobering - and scary - to come to the realization that when the wheels of my aircraft touched the runway in South Vietnam, it would be at least one year before I could return home - if I didn't die, that is. In that case, they would send me home sooner - in a box. Although I was confident in the training that I had received both in Basic and Signal School, I knew that the enemy was entrenched, and had already been at war for some time. There was still a lot about war that I had to learn. I was also aware that all of those guys who were being sent home in coffins had gone through roughly the same training that I got. It wasn't a good feeling. Was I scared? You betcha! I think we all were.

Entrance to the 244th company area.

Ready for bunker guard at Can Tho.

CHAPTER THREE

THE "DELTA HAWKS"

We flew the Polar Route from California, to Alaska, to Japan, to Vietnam. We landed in Vietnam at night. We had flown through part of a tropical storm , and had been bounced around some, so we were glad to be back on solid ground again - even if it was in a combat zone. The flare pots along the runway were doused quickly after we landed. No need to give the V.C. (VietCong) an easy target for their mortars or rockets.

As I headed down the aisle to the door of the aircraft, I saw that there was a stewardess (we call them flight attendants now) standing just inside the door, wishing us all good luck as we exited the plane. As I got near her, I said, "See you in a year!". I don't know how to describe the look that suddenly came on her face, but even though the light was dim, I thought that I could see something different about her eyes. Tears? Maybe - maybe not, but she was truly a professional, and she had obviously made this trip many, many times before. She shook my hand, and with what seemed to be much effort, she smiled at me and said, " Okay! I'll save you a seat!". I felt sorry for her then, because I realized that seeing young men off to war never gets easier, no matter how many times you do it.

The first thing that I noticed when I got off the plane was the smell. It wasn't a *bad* smell, but it was…*different.* It rather reminded me of that damp, woodsy smell that I remembered from those deep-in-the woods church camps that my folks used to send me to in the summer, except that there was the odor of diesel and jet fuel mixed with it. The humidity was high, so it seemed to magnify and mix a lot of different smells into one. Sometimes, I think I can *still* smell that smell. Strange, how you can remember little things like that.

During the next few days, we endured in-country processing, and then we were split up and sent to various units all across South Vietnam. About fifteen or twenty of us were loaded onto a military transport aircraft and flown to a place called Can Tho. We didn't have a clue where we were. We didn't know if we had been flown North - toward the D.M.Z (the Demilitarized Zone between North and South Vietnam), or South. I think we were all hoping for South. We knew that the closer you got to the D.M.Z., the heavier the fighting was, and we still weren't armed yet. Weapons weren't issued until you reached your final destination.

When we landed at Can Tho Army Airfield, we were taken to Battalion Headquarters for further processing. I was assigned to the 244th S.A.C. (Surveillance Aircraft Company), and led down to the company barracks area, where I found an empty bunk on the second floor. The barracks were divided into two-man rooms, so we did have some semblance of privacy - unlike Basic. I learned that I was sharing the room with a guy named Walt. He was a SP5(Specialist 5th class, almost a *god* to a lowly PFC) and had worked in the Avionics platoon for quite some time. He was a real nice guy, but the quiet type. He didn't talk much, but when he did, what he said was worth listening to. He really clued me in on how things worked - what to do, what not to do - stuff like that. We threw him a "short-time" party just before he finished his tour. That's when I found out the hard way that consumable alcohol and I don't mix. I still don't drink. Oh well, no great loss.

Walt led me down to the 244th Signal Platoon, where I met the Platoon Sergeant, and most of the guys that I would be working with. However, they were at a loss to tell me what my immediate duties would be since my M.O.S. was full. In short, they didn't need me! It was finally decided that I would be cross-trained on other electronic systems, like communication radios, radar altimeter, and later I even spent some time working nights in the Red Haze(infrared imaging) section.

I felt like a misfit from the very beginning, and I probably fit nearly all of the qualifications. Mostly - at first, anyway - I was mad for being trained to do a specific job, and then sent to a place where my skills weren't needed! I often wondered,

"What am I doing here?!". To my shame, I guess I really developed an "attitude" about my situation. As a result, no doubt, I was moved around a lot, as far as my duties were concerned. I was even temporarily assigned as an Orderly Room clerk, since I was one of the few guys in our unit who could type more than forty words per minute("Thank you, Mr. Joslyn!"). However, I eventually made it back to the avionics section.

The 244th was a surveillance aircraft company. We flew the Grumman OV-1 Mohawk. It was a two-man aircraft, with one pilot, and one T.O.(Technical Observer), who ran the cameras and other surveillance equipment. The "A" models had nose and belly cameras. The "B" models had S.L.A.R.(Side-Looking Airborne Radar) booms mounted underneath the fuselage. The "C" and "D" models usually flew Red Haze missions at night.

The Mohawk was a fully aerobatic aircraft. It had a tri-stabilizer tail, short stubby wings, and two huge turbo-prop engines. Actually, I'm not sure that it "flew", in the true sense of the word. I think it mostly just threw itself into the air - fast! It had two large auxiliary fuel tanks - one on the end of each wing, so it had a pretty good operating range, but it also had the glide ratio of a *brick!* In other words, if you lost one engine in flight, you'd better be looking for a place to land. If you lost both engines - well, I guess that's why it was the only Army aircraft at that time that had ejection seats. The pilot usually carried a sidearm, but the T.O. was unarmed. In fact, the aircraft itself was unarmed. It's a creepy feeling to know that people on the ground can shoot at you, but you can't shoot back.

Our unit was known as the Delta Hawks. "Delta", because Can Tho Army Airfield was located in the Mekong Delta. "Hawks", because we flew "Hawks" - Mohawks. We had a pretty good mission record, and as I recall, we only lost one aircraft and crew during my stay at the 244th.

Concerning that incident, a recovery team was sent out immediately to the crash site. They brought back a number of aircraft parts, and the human remains of the T.O.. However, according to eye witnesses in the area, the pilot had not ejected. So, the only task left was to locate and recover the pilot - or what was left of him, so he could be medically identified for government insurance purposes, and so that his family could be notified that he was officially K.I.A., rather than M.I.A.. Volunteers were needed for that part of the mission.

Now….my Dad, a W.W.II Veteran, probably gave me the best two pieces of advice that I ever got, concerning the military. Just before I climbed onto the bus to leave for Basic, he shook my hand, looked me in the eye, and said, "Just keep your eyes and ears open, and your mouth shut, and you'll do all right. Oh, and don't volunteer for anything." I think that's the first time I ever remember seeing tears in Dad's eyes. Well, I followed Dad's advice during Basic and Signal School, but in the case of this crash recovery, I volunteered to go. I guess that I felt we owed it to the pilot's family.

About thirty or so of us volunteers were loaded aboard a CH47 "Chinook" helicopter. The top of an old oil storage tank was cut off, and the rest of the tank, looking like a big skinny doughnut, was slung underneath the chopper. We found out what the tank was for when we arrived at the crash site. It was a rice paddy with about 30 inches of water on it. Somehow, it was determined approximately where the remains of the cockpit should be, so we hovered over that area and dropped the tank. It sank into the mud somewhat, and pretty much sealed out the water. After we were rid of the tank, the chopper flew off to the side a bit, then descended and let us all out. It reminded me of all the times back home that I had watched troops climbing out of the rear of a big chopper, on the evening news.

We had brought a life-raft with us, along with a gas-powered pump, hoses, some rations, and a couple of cases of soda to drink. We loaded the pump, hoses, and food into the life-raft, and waded over to the tank. We then hooked up the hoses, started the pump, and began pumping the water out of the tank. Meanwhile, the Chinook took off and left us there, to be picked up later. Myself and another guy were chosen to climb down into the tank and direct the hose until all of the water had been pumped out. The rest of the guys were spread out in a big circle to form a defensive perimeter around the tank.

When the water was gone, the pump was shut off, and we began digging with our hands in the mud. After about thirty minutes of this, my right foot suddenly sank about six inches, and some red stuff started rising to the surface. I put my fingers in it and lifted it to my nose, hoping that it didn't smell like blood. It didn't. It was JP4 jet fuel. We kept digging, and over the course of the next couple of hours we found a few small, mangled pieces of the aircraft, but nothing of the pilot. However, water was slowly beginning to seep back into the tank, and the jet fuel was floating on top of it. Both of us were feeling a stinging sensation in our feet by this time, so the officer in charge had us pump the tank dry again. We were then able to climb out of the tank to get a quick bite to eat. The officer then ordered us out to guard the perimeter, and two other guys were brought in to take our place in the tank. I think they were the ones who eventually found the medical evidence that we had been searching for.

I don't know how long we stood out there in that rice paddy, but the stinging in my feet had turned into a real burning sensation. By the time the Chinook arrived to pick us up, I was in some serious pain! The flight back to Can Tho seemed to take forever, and the pain got steadily worse as time went on. *Finally*, we landed, unloaded, and headed back to the barracks. I was limping by this time, and was looking forward to shedding my smelly, muddy fatigues - and especially the boots. After removing my grungy fatigues and boots, I slowly made my way down to the latrine to take a "bucket" shower. Even before I got to the latrine, my feet were beginning to swell, and had turned a very bright pink color. I took a good bucket shower, and by the time I returned to the barracks, blisters had begun to form on both of my feet, where my boots had been. The rest of my legs were a lighter shade of pink, *nearly* up to my groin. I put on clean clothing - except for socks and boots. The blisters were so big by now, that I couldn't get them on. I finally decided to try putting on my low quarters (dress shoes), *loosely* tied.

I then slowly headed in the direction of the Dispensary. An officer driving by in a Jeep stopped to bawl me out for being out of uniform, but when he saw the blisters on my ankles, he apologized many times over, and offered me a ride to the Dispensary. I gratefully accepted.

When I arrived at the Dispensary, I was questioned about how this had happened, and my feet and legs were examined. It was determined that I had suffered second degree chemical burns due to prolonged exposure to the jet fuel. They broke the blisters, peeled off the dead skin, put some kind of salve on the wounds, and wrapped it all in gauze. They gave me some pain pills, too, which were *greatly* appreciated.

Every time I changed position, like sitting up from lying in my bunk, or standing up from sitting down, all the blood in my body seemed to rush to my feet - and all those *raw* nerves there.

The pain was so intense, it was like being hit in the head with a sledge hammer, and nearly made me pass out. I likened it to standing over a blowtorch - barefooted. It was the most excruciating pain that I have ever endured in my life.

The routine continued for what seemed like many weeks. The bandages were changed every morning at the Dispensary, and they gave me more pain pills when I ran out. Eventually, the blisters quit forming, and I was able to bandage my feet by myself. Although my feet were still very tender, I was finally able to wear my jungle boots again. The scars, such as they were, came in the form of a darkening of the skin in some areas on my feet. It looked like the skin was "dirty" - like I never washed my feet. They lasted for several years, but gradually faded away, and there is no sign of them now. I also felt bad for the guy who was in the tank with me. His burns weren't as severe as mine, but we pretty much endured the same treatment - and the pain that went with it. Later, those of us on the recovery teams were awarded the Army Commendation Medal, with a written account of our "outstanding" efforts. No Purple Heart, though. Just purple feet.

Although I was in a strange place, far from home, I didn't really start to get lonely until around Thanksgiving and Christmas of 1969. Most of us spent our off-duty hours writing letters, reading and re-reading letters, playing "combat" volleyball (very few rules), or going to the E.M. Club to get a cool drink and listen to music. Many of us were also scouring the PACEX (Pacific Exchange) catalog for the latest in stereo and camera equipment. Believe it or not, I still have all of the stuff that I bought, and it all still works!

I got several big packages from home just before Christmas. One of them contained a miniature Christmas tree, complete with tiny ornaments, lights, and an angel on top. I also got cookies, fudge, and other Christmas candy. I enjoyed those packages tremendously, and was

27

comforted to know that the folks back home were missing me as much as I was missing them. I tried not to think about being lonesome, but sometimes we were all put in a situation where we didn't have much to do but think about or talk about home. I think that perimeter guard duty was the culprit here.

We were all required to pull guard duty on a regular basis. Sometimes it was a walking guard post, but usually we were put on bunker guard. There were 4-man bunkers set at strategic points around the perimeter of our airfield, and we were dropped off at the bunkers around 6:00 P.M., and picked up at about 6:00 A.M. Two of us would guard the bunker until midnight, and the other two would guard the rest of the shift. However, if needed, there were always four men available in each bunker, regardless of whose shift it was.

We had rations with us to eat, which we usually did about midnight. They weren't the fancy MRE's like the troops get nowadays, but they weren't too bad, if you could get past the taste. What made them taste bad was that nasty Army-issue mosquito repellant! We had to put it all over us, or we'd get eaten alive, but that stuff got onto and into *everything* - including the water in our canteen, our cigarettes, and our meal rations. It smelled about like burnt motor oil, and was every bit as oily on our skin.

We usually spent our time in the bunker watching the perimeter and visiting with each other about home and family. However, we could only talk about that stuff for so long without getting depressed about being separated from all of the people, places, and things that were familiar to us. Then, there were just long periods of silence.

That was when I would have hours and hours to just sit and *think*. Think about Gay. Think about my family. Think about my friends who were in college. Think about politics. Think about religion. It's amazing to me what questions you can ask yourself, and what answers you can come up with, when you have all of that time on your hands with nothing to do but sit and think about stuff.

Ever since I first learned that there was such

a thing as a rocket, I had wanted to be an astronaut. So I thought about that a lot, and what it might be like out there in space, or on some other planet, like Mars or Venus. I had also wanted to be an architect, so I thought about that, too. I drew house plans in my mind, and imagined what those homes would look like, if they were actually built. I also had a passion for inventing things, so I dreamed up numerous gadgets, what they would do, and how I would make them work. I'm *still* thinking about a couple of those machines, and they seem to have some promise, if I can somehow find the time and the money to build the prototypes. For instance, could you envision operating an automobile with a motor that doesn't consume anything that we presently consider to be "fuel"? Oh well, I'll let you know about that one.

One thing that I found myself thinking about a lot - at least, at first - was whether or not I could actually pull the trigger on another human being. I mean, if the enemy was right there in front of me, pointing his weapon at me, and I could see his (or her) face and his eyes, could I bring myself to pull the trigger before he did? I thought about asking Dad how he had handled this situation when he was in France during W.W. II, but he was a medic then, and he never talked about it much.

So, I decided to write to another former Maize High teacher, Mr. Ernest Smith, and tell him about my dilemma. I knew that Mr. Smith was also a veteran, and had fought in the European Theatre during W.W. II. I respected Mr. Smith very much (and still do), and I trusted him to give me good advice. Mr. Smith wrote back and told me that everyone who goes into combat eventually finds himself in the same situation. The words of his letter indirectly brought to memory something that I had been taught in Basic, but had somehow forgotten. We were told all during our training that there are only two kinds of soldiers on the battlefield – the *quick*, and the *dead*. Mr. Smith told me that when I was faced with that situation, however it might come about, he was sure that I would be able to do whatever was necessary. I felt better then, knowing that he had that much confidence in me to do my duty, as I was trained to do.

So, after many hours of contemplation, I finally decided that, yes, I could pull the trigger. After all, it wasn't *my* idea to go to Vietnam, and when I got there, it wasn't my intention to go looking for someone to kill as soon as I got off the plane. My intention was to help stop the North Vietnamese and Viet Cong from doing what they were doing to South Vietnam. All I wanted to do was do my job, help as much as I could, and go home alive and well. I reasoned that if I ever came face to face with the enemy, it would be because *he* was trying to kill *me.* In that scenario, I decided that I had better be quicker on the trigger, or me and some of my friends might be going home in a box.

Early in 1970, I was assigned to bunker guard duty during Tet - the Vietnamese New Year. I had a "boonie" hat by then, and I found it much more comfortable to wear on bunker guard, than the "steel pot" combat helmet. There was a R.V.N.

compound a short distance south of us, and the troops there were really celebrating Tet that particular night. From our bunker, we could see red tracer rounds flying into the air all over the place. We figured that they must have loaded their ammo clips with nothing but tracers, and fired them into the sky on full automatic. I guess it was the best they could do, in lieu of fireworks.

These outbursts were sporadic throughout the night, and started to worry us somewhat. After all, all of those bullets had to come down *somewhere*. We finally decided to take off our boonie hats and put on our steel helmets - just in case. I took off my hat and put it down on the edge of the bunker. When I leaned over to get my steel pot, I heard a "whizzing" noise, and my boonie hat went flying into the bunker! There was a small hole right in the top of it! We called the Sergeant of the Guard to report what had happened, but he wasn't surprised. It seems that ours was not the first bunker to receive "fallout". He told us to stay away from the edge of the bunker and hunker down for the rest of the night. No need to tell us twice, and *nobody* slept in our bunker that night!

Another thing that we thought about and discussed at length while on bunker guard duty, was how this war was being fought. *We* had "rules of engagement". The enemy didn't! Occasionally, through our Starlight scope, we could see someone moving around on the perimeter. It might be an innocent civilian who didn't get home before curfew (but not likely), or it might be Viet Cong setting up a mortar tube or a rocket launcher. Either way, we had to call the command bunker and get *permission* to fire even a warning shot!

After guard duty one night, I was so steamed that I fired off a letter to President Nixon. I asked him why we had rules, when the communists didn't. I asked him why we had to get permission to cover our own butts! I asked him if we had jumped in the pool to win this race, or were we just treading water? To my complete surprise, I actually got a reply to that letter! The envelope was addressed to me, with my correct APO number and everything, and the only return address was "The White House". WOW! I only knew of one place that had a return address like that!

As it turned out, the reply was written by one of President Nixon's aides, and pretty much laid out the administration's current policy on the Vietnam war. It more or less told me that we were not in Southeast Asia to annihilate North Vietnam. Rather, we were there to protect South Vietnam. It was also explained to me that if we stooped to the enemy's level, we wouldn't be any better than he is. Whatever! To my way of thinking, if you go to war, you'd better be going in to win, because if you're not going in to win, you're going in to lose. There isn't really much of an in-between.

I would use the sandlot baseball analogy here. Let's say that you are the biggest kid on the block, with the biggest bat on the block. You are capable of hitting a home run almost at will. However, if the opposing team knows that you're too afraid of a certain pitch to stay in the batter's box, then they will just keep throwing that same pitch. You'll never even swing that big bat. To them, you're no threat at the plate. You're just an "easy out". I guess what I'm trying to say is this: If we, as a country, make the decision to step into that big international batter's box, we had better be ready, willing, and able to swing our big bat and stay in the box until we either get a hit, a run, or strike out - regardless of who is pitching! The letter that I had received from the White House didn't give me all of the answers that I was looking for, but I realized that it was all I would get, and would have to be satisfied with that.

After five or six months at Can Tho, I pretty much had the routine down. I had learned a few words and simple phrases in Vietnamese, but nothing that would qualify me as bilingual, and I remember very little of it now. Daily life wasn't too bad overall, and we hadn't been "hit" since I got there. I was saving money for the upcoming wedding and honeymoon, and I wanted to buy a new car, too.

That's when I decided to extend my tour.

We could extend our initial tour for six months at a time. For that, we got extra leave, and an extra R&R (Rest and Recuperation). Besides, Stateside pay didn't compare very well with Combat pay, and I didn't really feel like I was in mortal danger every minute of every day. I was fortunate. I had it easy, compared to many who served in Vietnam. For some of them, almost every day was a living Hell.

Of course, as soon as my extension papers came through, we started taking mortars. The V. C. really *hated* our unit. Our Mohawks equipped with infrared would sometimes fly cooperative missions with the 235th Assault Helicopter Company (Cobras). We would find the enemy enemy moving at night, radio the coordinates back to the 235th, and their Cobras would take care of the problem. Without the Delta Hawks, the V.C. didn't have to worry much about making large troop movements at night.

As a consequence, we started getting mortared. By "we", I mean *our unit.* There were all kinds of units at Can Tho - MedEvac, Chinooks,

Hueys, Cobras, and of course, Mohawks. The first time we took mortars, the V.C. really zeroed in on *us*. They lobbed in quite a few rounds, several landing in front of our maintenance hangars, a couple in front of the Orderly Room - skipped over the M.A.R.S. station(2-way radio communications) and the U.S.O. Club - and placed at least one mortar on or between the next four barracks. *Our* barracks. Fortunately, no one was killed, but the barracks next to mine was hit, and six guys were sent to Japan for surgery and recovery. The V.C. were sending us a message. We got the message, but we still had a job to do, and our mission didn't change.

When extending a tour, we had the option of taking our free 30-day leave up to sixty days prior, or sixty days after our previously scheduled departure date. I had received word that my Grandma Dundas had suffered a severe heart attack, and was in the hospital trying to recover. It was really bad for her. I was scheduled to return to the States in early August, 1970, but I decided to take the "sixty days prior" option, in case Grandma should take a sudden turn for the worse.

I called Gay via the M.A.R.S. station, and told her that I would be coming home in early June, instead of August. She was already upset about my tour extension, as was my whole family, but when I told her why I had decided take my extension leave early, she understood. She then asked me, "So, do you still want get married when you come home, even though you have to go back?" My answer was definitely "YES!". I guess that I didn't think about how much work it would be for her to put together a wedding in less than 30 days. She got it all set, up, though, I think with much help from family and friends. It would turn out to be a terrific event!

Me at work - 244th Red Haze section

Me again, flying as T.O. on a daytime photo
mission

On the flight line at Can Tho.

Suited up to fly.

Barracks next to mine, after mortar attack.

CHAPTER FOUR

HOME ON LEAVE

I landed in Wichita, Kansas in early June, 1970. I was met at the airport by Gay and both of our families. It was GREAT! During the next couple of weeks, Gay and I set out to finish the arrangements for our upcoming wedding - which included taking delivery on our new car! I had sent my folks the down-payment money to order it, and it came in early. It was a Dodge Charger 500 SE. It was a light gold color, with a black vinyl top, black leather high-backed bucket seats, a 383 Magnum V8 engine, floor shift, European-style mag wheels, racing gas cap, and hood pins. It even had a "real live" 8-track stereo. It only averaged about eleven miles to the gallon (on premium fuel), but gas was only about 19 cents a gallon back then, so it was no big deal. It was a *beautiful* machine! Wish I still had it.

Finally, the big day came - June 28, 1970.

My Best Man, C.D. Sullard, and all of the groomsmen jokingly tried to talk me out of "taking the plunge", but they knew that wasn't going to happen. Everything went smoothly until I saw Gay coming down the aisle on her dad's arm. I nearly lost it. I already knew that she was beautiful, but - *WOW!* We said our vows, special music was performed, and then we had "the big kiss", and made the traditional walk back down the aisle - for the first time as Mr. and Mrs. . I felt like the luckiest guy in the world! Still do.

There was the reception, with cake, punch, gifts, and all that goes with it - pictures, too. Fun! Then there was the rice-throwing, the "getaway", and we headed off on our honeymoon in the new car. Our original honeymoon plans got messed up a bit, but we didn't care. All we knew or cared about was the fact that we were finally together, and we had a WEEK alone to get used to the idea of being husband and wife. We rented a small cabin on Grand Lake, and had a *wonderful* time!

After returning from our honeymoon, we

spent about a week with my folks, and about the same with Gay's folks. We also visited Grandma in the hospital. She almost seemed to be back to her old self. She was upset about having to miss our wedding, but was otherwise in good spirits - laughing and joking as always. Sadly, she passed away in her sleep the night before she was due to be released from the hospital. I was a pallbearer at her funeral.

Grandma(Martha) Dundas was laid to rest in Enid, Oklahoma, next to Grandpa(Basil Rudolph Dundas, Sr.). Following the funeral and graveside service, the family gathered together to visit, recall the good times we'd had at Grandma's house, and generally get re-acquainted with each other. I was visiting with my cousin, Richard, when he asked me to step out behind the house with him for a few minutes. He said it was *important.* The solemn look on his face told me that he was dead serious. He told me that he had to get something out of his car, and he'd meet me behind the house shortly.

I went into the back yard, and when Richard

arrived, he was carrying a Boy Scout hatchet, and a new deck of playing cards. He broke the seal on the box, removed the cards, and separated the Ace of Spades from the rest of the deck. He handed me the Ace, and proceeded to chop the rest of the deck in half with the hatchet. Then he said, " The Ace that you have is the only thing left of this deck. The rest of it is now worthless. It's for good luck. Promise me that you'll take it with you when you go back to Vietnam, and promise me that you'll bring it back to me, okay?" I promised.

I could tell that the little ritual he had performed meant a lot to Richard, and even though I am not a superstitious person, it meant a lot to me, too. I still carry that Ace in my wallet. I haven't seen Richard for quite some time now, but as long as I still have the Ace, I know that we will always be somehow connected.

It was hard enough, knowing that my leave was coming to an end but losing Grandma so suddenly made it much harder. I was already apprehensive about returning to 'Nam and leaving

48

my family, my friends, and especially my new wife - again. I was going back to the 244th, though, so I knew that I would be in familiar territory. I kept assuring Gay and everyone else that I would be all right, but that didn't make leaving any easier. I kept remembering Dad's words, "...and don't volunteer for anything. " Oh, well – too late. Besides, I had no way of knowing just how different things would be when I returned to Can Tho.

CHAPTER FIVE

BACK TO THE R. V. N.

It's strange how that when we return to a certain place after being away for an extended period of time, we always expect everything to be exactly the same as it was when we left. Deep down, we know that the people we know and the places that are familiar will change in our absence, but we still expect them to stay the same, because that's the way these things are remembered. It's the way we *want* them to be.

Home was not the same when I got there on leave. My siblings were nearly a year older. My sister, Susie, had graduated from Maize High School. Brother Mark and sister Laurie were growing like weeds. A few new houses were going up in Maize. Many of my friends were either taking summer school for college, or had jobs to help pay for the Fall semester. All of these things were still good - but not the same.

GLAD YOU'RE BACK!

When I returned to Can Tho, it wasn't the same either. My old unit, the 244th, was being deactivated. Nearly all of the aircraft were gone - transferred to other Mohawk units in South Vietnam. With them went the pilots, flight crews, maintenance personnel - nearly everybody. The barracks area almost looked like a ghost town. The few people who were left, were tying up the loose ends before they left for their new assignments. Talk about *depressing!*

A couple of months before I went home on leave, the rumor mill (the military *always* has rumors) had it that the 244th and several other units at Can Tho might be deactivated as part of the "Vietnamesation" program. We would sit around the barracks at night, speculating about how this might happen. We dreamed about our Mohawks being flown to a South Vietnamese port city, seeing them lifted out to a waiting aircraft carrier or large Navy transport ship - and us going with them. We would then make the long, lazy journey by sea back to *"the WORLD"* - that's what we called the United States. It wasn't the *whole* world, but it was *our* world. Yes, it would be great to be reassigned Stateside for the rest of the war. It was a nice dream, but that's all it was and ever would be - a dream.

I was reassigned to the 73rd S.A.C., another Mohawk unit, located at a place called Long Thanh North. I had absolutely no idea where that was, but the word "north" gave me a chill. All I knew (or thought I knew) was that if I was going North, I would be closer to where the *real* fighting was going on. In truth, the *real* fighting was wherever the enemy happened to be, and you never really knew where that was for sure.

When I asked where Long Thanh North was, the guy sending me there said, "Well, I'm not real certain, but I think it's a little airfield about thirty miles East of Saigon.". Saigon? Saigon! Man, we had heard horror stories about the V.C. activity in and around Saigon! As it turned out, my fears were for the most part unwarranted.

Before we go any further here, I want to

make something *very* clear. I am quite aware that the city which I refer to as Saigon has been renamed. However, I am not "politically correct" enough to refer to it by its' new name. Hope I never am. I remember it as Saigon, and to me it *always* will be Saigon - and still *should* be.

I settled in at Long Thanh and the 73rd easier than I had expected. I was quickly put to work in the Nav. van of the Avionics Platoon. I was finally working the M.O.S. that I had trained for at Signal School! We didn't live in barracks at Long Thanh, but rather in one-floor, eight-man dwellings with sandbags stacked around them. We called them "hooches". The showers were still down the way a bit, but they had real running water, so it was "goodbye" to the days of the bucket shower! There was an E. M. Club, too, and a makeshift outdoor movie theater. It usually showed the same movie every night for a week, but so what? It was a movie! Of course, we didn't always have time for the club or the movie theater, but it was nice to know that they were available. I was beginning to think that maybe this place wasn't as bad as I had thought it would be.

Our Commanding Officer, Major Ivan L. Waggoner, was pretty cool, I thought. He was a 1962 West Point graduate, and although he was very businesslike and methodical in the way that he ran his command, he seemed to me to be a bit more "laid back" than a couple of other W.P. grads I had previously run across. At least, if you were called to the Orderly Room for something, you didn't automatically feel like you were heading for a courts martial. He set up a company "bitch hour" every week. Once a week (on Mondays, I think), we could sign in with the First Sergeant, wait our turn, and then go into the C.O.'s office. Once the door was shut, we could say anything we wanted to - *off the record.* I think that was a pretty smart move on Major Waggoner's part. It allowed the men to vent some steam and release their frustrations, which reduced tension in the unit. The C.O. could also get a realistic view of the morale of his men, find out what was bothering them the most, and either initiate changes to help the situation, or explain to them why he couldn't fix all of their problems. Besides, this way, the men could find out where the C.O. was coming from, too. It was hard for some of the guys to understand that even the boss had a boss. And so did *his* boss - you get the idea.

All in all, life at the 73rd wasn't too bad. We were kept busy with trying to keep the avionics equipment working in all of our aircraft. Heat, humidity, and dirt don't mix well with electronic components. Sometimes I would work on the equipment in the Nav. van, but other times I would have to troubleshoot problems with the equipment still installed in the aircraft. That meant going out on the flight line, and working on the aircraft while they were parked in the revetments. Sometimes, the crew chief would run up one of the engines, so I could test the equipment while it was operating on aircraft power, rather than an A.P.U.(Auxiliary Power Unit). It was *really* noisy, and you really had to watch out for the propellers. You got used to it.

You had to be careful not to get *too* used to it, though, or you could accidentally walk right into a propeller. I know that sounds crazy, but it happened far too often in Vietnam. Guys would get accustomed to working on aircraft out on the flight line, and somehow forget that they were running. There were those who lost their lives by walking into a turning propeller, or the tail rotor of a chopper. I was nearly one of them.

Once when I was working the night shift in the Red Haze section at the 244th in Can Tho, one of our Mohawks took off, circled the field, and landed. The pilot radioed that there was something wrong with the infrared. I met him at the flight line, and over the noise of the engines, he described the problem they were having. Based on that information, I was sure that I knew where the little black box was that controlled that function. It was in the fuselage on the pilot's side of the aircraft, under the left wing. That's all I had on my mind when I turned and headed in that direction.

Suddenly, I felt a rush of air not too far from

my head. I froze! *Slowly*, I turned my head to look over my left shoulder. The pilot, God bless him, was hanging half way out of the cockpit, with his arm stretched out - reaching for me. Very slowly, I lowered myself to my knees, crawled over to retrieve the black box, and exited to the rear of the aircraft. I ran to the Red Haze van, got a replacement part, and returned to the ramp. After quickly installing the new part, I went around the left wing and up to the cockpit. I informed the pilot that the system should work now. I also tried to thank him for what he had tried to do for me, but with the engine noise, I'm not sure that he heard all that I was saying. He just looked at me, slowly turned his head from side to side, then gave me the "thumbs up" sign. After I had backed away from the aircraft, he closed the cockpit, taxied back to the runway, and flew off into the darkness.

I stood there, watching until the aircraft running lights were shut off, and I couldn't hear the engines any more. It seemed very quiet then, even though I could still hear chopper blades beating the air, as our patrol chopper circled the airfield. You could hear helicopters twenty-four hours a day at Can Tho, but they seemed somehow distant at that moment.

I guess that's when the fear factor finally kicked in, and I began to realize the gravity of what had just happened - and what had *almost* happened. My knees went weak, and I began to shake. I didn't know whether to laugh, cry, pass out, or just sit down. I sat down - right out there in the middle of nowhere on the flight ramp. I didn't realize that there were tears in my eyes until my vision became blurry. I have absolutely no idea how long I sat out there in the darkness before I recovered enough to return to the van. That was far and away the most frightened that I have ever been, or ever want to be again.

We experienced a similar incident while I was at the 73rd, only this time it was fatal. Our new maintenance officer, a captain (and also a pilot), had gone up on a mission, flying as T.O., to get checked out on procedures for flying the surveillance missions. Upon returning to Long Thanh, they lowered the landing gear, but got a "No Lock" light on the right landing gear. They cycled the gear several times, and even though it was confirmed that the gear was down, the warning light persisted. The decision was made to divert them to Bien Hoa Air Force Base, where they could attempt a landing after the runway had been foamed.

The report that we received indicated that the actual landing went fine. The right landing gear held. When the aircraft came to a stop, the Captain immediately exited the aircraft - even though the pilot was yelling at him not to get out until the engines were shut down. Too late. The Captain had already unplugged his flight helmet, and didn't hear the warning.

Witnesses reported that while the pilot was shutting down the engines as quickly as possible, the Captain walked around the right wing of the aircraft and retrieved a lock pin from a maintenance door in the fuselage. He inserted the pin in the right landing gear to ensure that it wouldn't collapse, then walked toward the front of the aircraft - right into the still-turning propeller.

The Captain's sudden death came as a shock to all of us. He had been with us only a short time, but seemed to be well-liked by nearly everyone. I had talked to him briefly only a couple of times, but he seemed to be a really nice guy.

We had a memorial ceremony on the flight ramp, in his honor. The other pilots and officers were pretty torn up - especially the Warrant Officer who was piloting the Mohawk on the day of the accident. Not only had he been present to witness this tragedy, but he and the Captain shared the same last name. It was very, very hard on him.

Unfortunately, we would lose other pilots and T.O.'s during my stay at Long Thanh North, but they flew a different type of aircraft. They were officially designated as the YO-3A, but we called them "Yo-Yo's". I think they operated at a higher altitude than the Mohawks, but they flew much, much slower, and were whisper quiet. If a Yo-Yo was flying over your head at an altitude of only 100 feet, you might not even know it was there, unless you just happened to look up. They were that quiet. After losing two or three crews, the Yo-Yo's were grounded, pending an investigation. I don't know if they ever flew again while I was at Long Thanh.

One problem that we had both at Can Tho and at Long Thanh was racism. It was pretty one-sided, though. You have to understand that all this was happening during the era of the Civil Rights movement. I didn't really notice too much racial tension during Basic or Signal School. We didn't have time then for such nonsense, and the military simply didn't tolerate that type of behavior - at least, not in the States.

Vietnam was a different story. The Black Panthers were very prevalent in 'Nam. They would walk around with a clenched fist in the air - the "Black Power" salute - and *dare* anyone to say something about it. They also had their "30-minute handshake", and "the *walk*". It was sometimes hilarious to watch, but contributed to the racial tension nevertheless. It didn't help when some of the guys from the South started hanging Rebel flags in their hooches, and when the white guys started copying the "brothers' " handshake, it made matters even worse. The white guys thought it was funny, but the Brothers didn't, so they kept changing it - often.

What bothered me most about the Panther activity was that it was dividing our units into groups, rather than allowing us to do our jobs *together*. In one incident, a big fight broke out just down the airfield from the 73rd. Rumor had it that a couple of guys were actually killed! Of course, we could never confirm that - officially. The Army wasn't talking, but that was for morale purposes, I suppose. Nevertheless, when I heard the rumor, I was absolutely *livid!* I was mad at *both* sides for letting the situation get to that point. I mean - had we traveled half-way around the world just to fight *each other?* How crazy is THAT? We were all supposed to be on the same side, you know? It was all so ridiculous that it still makes me mad when I think about it.

I had made friends with a couple of black guys in the Avionics platoon, but outside of work we really didn't fraternize much. It was as much for their safety as mine. The Brothers frowned heavily on blacks being friendly with white guys, especially in public. It was a shame, because these black friends of mine were pretty nice guys. I felt sorry for them because of the pressure they were under, so I didn't take offense if they avoided me in public. To help ease the situation, I decided just not to approach them outside of work. I didn't ignore them, but I didn't initiate a public conversation, either. I told them privately why I maybe didn't seem quite as friendly outside the workplace, and they both understood. I think they were also relieved. After all, the Panthers were out to make a statement, and if you disagreed or just didn't want to go along with that statement, you could actually be physically injured - no matter what color you skin was. It *was* that bad!

Don't misunderstand me. I didn't blame *all* of the racial tension on the Black Panthers. I'm not that stupid or naïve. There were groups on both sides of the issue. I guess that I was in the group that didn't care to be part of any of the other groups. I was just as disgusted by the KKK and what they claim to stand for, as I was by the Panthers and their agenda.

Also, I have a feeling that the type and degree of racism that I witnessed was more prevalent in the so-called "rear areas", or support units like ours. Out in the field, where the troops were meeting the enemy face-to-face on a daily basis, I don't think that they had a lot of idle time to sit around and ponder social issues. They were mostly just trying to survive, and they had to trust and depend on each other daily for that survival. They were, I think, more concerned with just doing their job, finishing their tour, and *going home* in one piece.

I just feel that where I was, and at that time, the Panthers' activities and attitude simply contributed to making an already bad situation even worse. As the old saying goes, "I call'em like I see'em", and where I was, and when I was there, that's how I saw it. Some may disagree with my assessment of the situation, but that doesn't really bother me. Everyone has the right to disagree, but that won't change anything that happened to me or how I feel about it.

I felt then, as I still do, that we Americans have enough problems to try to solve. Wondering about where our ancestors came from, or worrying about the color of a person's skin should not be among them. We citizens of the United States are *all* supposed to be AMERICANS. Isn't that enough?

CHAPTER SIX

THE ENEMY

We called them "Charlie". It was our nickname for the Viet Cong, or V.C.. There were the North Vietnamese regulars, too. And the kids.

The North Vietnamese were well-trained and well-equipped by their Red Chinese and Soviet "advisors" in all aspects of warfare - military and political strategy, and psychological warfare. I think that most Americans looked upon the Vietnamese as a socially and economically backward culture compared to ours, and perhaps in many ways that was true. However, *backward* does not mean *stupid*. These people learn very quickly, and are very adept at absorbing information and utilizing that which suits their needs.

As for Charlie's motivation, the communist propaganda machine had a lot to do with that. Failure of a mission could result in imprisonment, torture, or even death for those involved *and* their family members. When these are the only options, you get a highly motivated fighting force. The North Vietnamese had studied world history, and learned from it. They took pages from the books of people like Hitler, Tojo, Stalin, and Mao, and used them to their advantage. Yes, fear from within is a great motivator.

The V.C. were trained in guerrilla warfare by their North Vietnamese counterparts, and could sneak in and out of secure installations with relative ease. There were many South Vietnamese civilian workers on all of the military bases. Usually these were the "Mama-Sans" who cleaned our barracks, washed our clothes, and polished our boots. Some worked at the mess hall, or waited tables at the clubs. We paid "X" dollars per month to a civilian agency, and the workers were paid in Piasters - Vietnamese currency. The mama-sans took pretty good care of us, so we were freed up to do our military jobs, rather than having to spend time doing laundry and such. This arrangement helped us, and put money into the South Vietnamese economy via the wages that the civilian workers received. They would always come on post in the morning, or early afternoon, and leave in the evening before curfew.

Many of these civilian workers were also Viet Cong. They would perform their mundane duties on post each day, all the while gathering bits and pieces of potentially useful information to pass on to their V.C. friends.

At Long Thanh, it was noticed that one elderly papa-san was sweeping along the edge of the flight ramp. He swept up and down the edge of the ramp several times, and came under suspicion when someone finally realized that *nobody* sweeps the ramp! After being detained and questioned, it was learned that he was actually pacing off the distance between certain points along the ramp, so the V.C. could more accurately aim their mortars for a planned future attack. We heard that he broke down, crying, during the interrogation. He explained that he had no choice in doing what he did. The local V.C. had threatened to kill his family if he didn't do as he was told. He could have been lying, but that was the type of tactics that Charlie used quite often, and quite effectively. We never did learn whatever happened to the old guy.

The V.C. would use the same type of tactic with kids. You couldn't blame the kids too much, but that didn't make them any less dangerous. I mean, if Charlie cornered an eight or ten year old boy and gave him a job to do, and told him that they would torture and kill his father, mother, and siblings if he didn't do it - what's he going to say, "No"? I don't think so.

He would do as he was told, thinking that he was protecting his family. More often than not, he would complete his task, return to the place that he called home, and find his family murdered anyway. Then he was either an orphan left to fend for himself, or he might also be executed to ensure his silence. No big deal to Charlie. There were always lots of kids around. This boy would just become another statistic. Nasty people, those V.C.

Many of us viewed the American (or any other) media personnel as our enemy. That may sound a little nuts, but we had good reason to dislike them. People died because of them.

Don't misunderstand me. I *do* believe in the First Amendment - freedom of speech, the citizen's "right to know", and all of that. However, I don't necessarily believe that just because we have the *right* to know, we always have a *need* to know. What many in the media didn't understand then, and often still don't understand, is that when you report something to the American public, you are, in effect, telling *everyone* what you know - even the enemy. Our enemies can read, and they can watch the news on T.V., too. They can save a fortune on intelligence-gathering, if all they have to do is pick up a newspaper or turn on the evening news to find out what they want to know.

The old W.W.II slogan, "loose lips sink ships", still holds true. At least the media of that era knew that there were things that should not be made public if it would put American or Allied lives at risk. Much of what we know about the planning and operations conducted during W.W.II were made public only *after* the war was over. There may be a lot that we still don't know.

Let me put this into perspective concerning the war in Vietnam. Let's assume that one morning you pick up your newspaper, or turn on your T.V., and either read, or see and hear this report:

"The Can Tho Army Airfield came under a short mortar attack last night. Little damage and only minor injuries were reported, with no fatalities."

This would seem to be a reasonably accurate and innocent-sounding report, right? Nobody died, although those six guys that were sent to Japan for medical treatment might have a problem with the "only minor injuries" part. The mortar craters were filled in, and the damaged buildings were repaired. No harm done with that report, right? WRONG!

What that report told the Viet Cong was this:

1. They didn't do as much damage as they had planned.

2. They didn't hurt or kill enough people.

3. They needed to adjust their mortars for better accuracy.

4. They needed to hit us again.

And they *did* hit us again - several times.

I seem to recall reading about an American movie actress who visited North Vietnam during the war. Of course, the media was all over that visit like bees on honey. It was supposed to be a peace mission, or "mission of good will" - something like that. She was allowed to see several of our P.O.W.'s who were being held at the "Hanoi Hilton" prison camp. The prisoners were cleaned up, given a few decent meals, and clean prison uniforms in anticipation of her visit. As they shook hands with her, they passed her small notes, telling how they were *really* being treated. She reportedly took each note without flinching, and without looking at them, handed the notes over to the North Vietnamese officer who was accompanying her.

After she left, all of those P.O.W.'s were beaten mercilessly. As a result of the beatings, several of those brave men died. They had trusted her to take the *truth* back to the American people, and made the ultimate sacrifice for their attempt.

I don't recall seeing anything in the news about *that.* I think that those details were only made public after the P.O.W.'s were released, and somebody wrote a book about it all. I understand that she eventually apologized, but that won't bring those brave men back. Besides, I often wonder how you would actually go about making an apology to a dead man?

Naturally, the world-wide media really played up her visit. The North Vietnamese were particularly pleased with the press coverage. Once again, they had successfully manipulated the media to further their agenda, and influence the American public to push for a quicker pull-out. They were very good at that.

One of their tactics was to build anti-aircraft gun emplacements, missile batteries, and other military installations close to hospitals, orphanages, etc.. That way, when our B-52's bombed military targets, the communists could call in the world press and demonstrate to them how the "evil and heartless capitalist Americans" were dropping bombs on children, the sick, and the elderly! Their propaganda machine was *always* in high gear. Probably still is.

The U.S. didn't have the pinpoint accuracy "smart" bombs then, like we do today, although we were working in that direction. No doubt there were innocent people who lost their lives during our bombing campaign over North Vietnam. As badly as we feel about their loss, we must remember that it was their own government who put them in harm's way - on purpose - to use their deaths as propaganda. Those poor people were the innocent victims of a war that their own cruel government had initiated. They call *us* evil?

Eventually, because of political and social pressure that I believe was largely influenced by the left-wing media, we were forced to announce a timed withdrawal from South Vietnam. Big mistake. I'm no expert on military strategy, but I believe that most of those who *are* will agree with me on the following:

Even if the enemy knows that you are planning to invade his territory, it's not really a big deal as long as he understands, in no uncertain terms, that there is absolutely no way he can stop you. However, you never tell him *when* you're coming. Also, and just as important, when planning a troop reduction or withdrawal, you never, never, *never* tell him *when* you're leaving! That gives the enemy at least three options:

1. He can continue doing what he's doing.

2. He can step up what he's doing to "encourage" you to leave sooner.

3. He can just lay low, wait until you've left, and then walk in and take over.

I also feel very strongly that those so-called "arm-chair generals" in Congress should not try to tell our military *how* to do its' job. I believe that once our military forces have been committed to an operation, we should stand back and let them do what they do best. Our military commanders are experts at what they do. They will let us know what they require in manpower, equipment, and logistic support to successfully accomplish their mission. They will give us progress reports, and they will tell us when the mission is completed - however long that takes. That is what we pay them for, and they do it better than anyone else in the world.

As civilians, we need to give our military the resources that they require, the moral support that they deserve, and otherwise stay out of their way - and *be patient*. None of this "I support our troops, but not the war" nonsense. You can't have it both ways. These are lessons that we should have learned in Vietnam. I thought maybe we had.

However, when I watch the nightly news, or read the newspapers these days, I get the unpleasant feeling that most of the American media and a goodly number of our elected representatives in Washington, D.C. have failed American History! Let's not go there......*again.*

H E R O E S

We usually think of heroes as ordinary people who exhibit extraordinary bravery, like Alvin York in W.W.I, or Audie Murphy in W.W.II. I consider all Congressional Medal of Honor recipients to be heroes. There are others, though.

Consider the brave P.O.W.'s. These people not only did their military job, but endured mental and physical abuse at the hands of their captors. Most of them survived the ordeal. Some did not.

Consider those who went to war and did their job, then volunteered their spare time (if any) to work in orphanages or medical facilities, or used their talents to teach an illiterate person to read.

Consider the doctors who saw firsthand the aftermath of battle, and labored above and beyond the call of duty to save lives - and the heartbreak and frustration that they felt when they couldn't.

Consider those nurses who assisted in surgery, tended to the injuries of the wounded, and also took the time to try to comfort their patients emotionally as well.

Consider the pilots and crews of the MedEvac choppers who risked their lives on a regular basis to land, often while under fire themselves, to evacuate the wounded.

Consider all of those Army, Navy, Air Force, Marine, and Coast Guard personnel who put themselves and their machines in harm's way to deter an enemy attack, or to rescue civilians.

Consider also, those who served with the U.S.O. - people who gave of their time and talents to travel half-way around the world, and bring a little bit of home to those of us serving in a combat zone. They did this for us, knowing full well that they could also become casualties of war. They were heroes, too - and there are still others.

Not all of the heroes actually went to the combat zone, or even wore a military uniform.

Many of the heroes were those who stayed home and desperately tried to make things work while their loved ones were gone to war. They were the parents, wives, children, siblings, and fiancees who sent packages, wrote letters of encouragement, took an extra job to pay the bills, and *waited.* They were the ones who had to watch the casualty figures on the evening news each night - always hoping that their loved one was not among the statistics. They were the ones who had to deal with death when a couple of officers in military dress uniform came knocking at their door.

I found out many years after the war, that my youngest sister, Laurie, had refused to watch the television news while I was in South Vietnam. She was only eight or nine years old at the time, and she was afraid that if she watched the news, she would see my name listed among those Killed In Action. She knew that the actual names were not shown on T.V. - only the numbers - but it still scared her. I guess that by not watching the news, it was her way of helping to keep her big brother safe. What a thing for a child to have to go through! I'm sure that she was only one of many, many children who had similar feelings, but when she finally told me about how she felt back then, I cried anyway. We both did. It was personal.

Many times the efforts put forth by those who were still back in the *world* were nothing short of heroic. Not only did they have to deal with having a loved one serving in Vietnam, but still had to go through the daily routine of work, school, church, etc. - just like all of the *normal* people around them. Life was hard for these people, counting the days until that Vietnam returnee showed up at the bus station, train depot, or airport. It was even harder when that person *didn't* come home - not alive, anyway. Heroes? Yes, these people were heroes too.

By my own definition of the word "hero", I do not qualify. I'm not a coward, either, but I certainly do not consider myself a hero. I don't meet the criteria. However, I do know one Vietnam War hero quite well. I am married to her.

During my time in Vietnam and after, Gay has put up with more from me than any one person should have to - not only because of things that happened, but also because of things that *didn't* happen because of the war. She has been a real trooper through all these years. She would listen when I felt like talking. She understood when I didn't want to talk about the war. She never asked me questions that she felt I might not want to answer. Because of her example and her patience, I finally started going to church, and eventually became a Christian. Gay is *my* hero.

In front of our hooch at the 73rd-Long Than North

GLAD YOU'RE BACK!

SHORT!

CHAPTER EIGHT

COMING HOME

Life at Long Thanh was overall better than at Can Tho, but the day-to-day monotony of trying to keep our Mohawks flying regular missions just seem to make the time *drag*. We all had "short-time" calendars, where we could mark off each day until it was time to go back to the *world*, but even that didn't help much.

All during my tours in Vietnam, the family was really great about keeping in touch. Gay usually hand wrote letters. My Mom was especially good about sending taped letters. Whenever there was a family gathering, she would turn on the recorder and tape the singing, laughing, and just general conversation. Toward the end of the tape, Susie, Mark, and Laurie would send me a personal message, and Mom and Dad always had things to say, too. Dad usually closed his part of the tape with, "Keep your head down!".

The letters and tapes usually made me a little homesick, but it was great to hear from everyone anyway. It let me know that half-way around the planet, the *world* was still there, and I was looking forward to seeing it again before too long.

I must admit that I wasn't too good about writing letters, though. Mostly, it was because it would have been a repeat of the same old stuff. Other times, it was because there were things happening that I didn't want the folks at home to know about. They were worried enough as it was.

In December, 1970, we got word that the Bob Hope USO Christmas Show would be coming to Long Binh, which wasn't very far from Long Thanh North. Once in a while, several of us were able to borrow a ¾ ton truck and make the trip to Long Binh to visit the big PX there. Since we already knew the way to Long Binh, and we had all of our work caught up, we begged for permission to go to this big event. Finally, permission was granted, so on the big day, we got a truck and headed for Long Binh. It was only about a 20 or 25 mile drive, but it seemed to take *forever.*

When we arrived, we couldn't believe how many people were already there, and they were from all branches of the military. Our small group was so far from the stage that I had to use the zoom lens on my camera to try to see who was who. When Bob Hope came on stage he was carrying a golf club, and he got a standing ovation. I remember his opening line. He said, "Well, here we are in Long Binh. Long Binh - 'sounds like a description of Dean Martin's wine cellar!" The crowd erupted in laughter, and the show was under way! It was a terrific show, with singers, dancers, and of course, Bob Hope's jokes. It all ended too soon for us, though, and we made our way back to Long Thanh to resume our duties with the 73rd. That show gave us all a big lift, and we talked about it for months afterward. We'd had a great time that short afternoon, but in the long run, it was still just one of many days that were spent far from home.

In January, 1971, Gay and I met in Hawaii for a week of R&R. We spent the week just enjoying each other, and seeing some of the sights on Oahu. Visiting the U.S.S. Arizona memorial was emotional for both of us, but mostly we just had fun. It was a wonderful week, but it passed much too quickly. It's no wonder that she got upset when I extended my tour a second time (I told you that she put up with a lot from me).

The Army had an "early-out" program at the time, which allowed anyone returning from Vietnam with 150 days or less of active duty left on their enlistment , to be released from active duty immediately upon their return. I extended my tour just enough to meet the criteria. My total time in Vietnam turned out to be one year, eleven months, and eighteen days - not that I was counting. Well, we were *all* actually counting. As I mentioned previously, we had our short-time calendars, where we marked off each day until DEROS (Date Estimated Return from OverSeas). When we got down to sixty days, we took great pleasure in just blurting out, "SHORT!", no matter where we were, and for no particular reason. When we got down to thirty days, we considered ourselves to be so short that we would have had to parachute off the edge of a dime!

Long Thanh North was located east of Saigon, Long Binh, and Bien Hoa, so for months we had been watching big jet liners pass overhead, flying to and from those places. The aircraft flying west were carrying our replacements, we hoped, and the ones flying east were going back to the *world*! We called them "Freedom Birds", and we knew that one day soon we would be on one of them.

In May, 1971, I received a very disturbing message. My uncle, Paul Reynard, a Captain in the Air Force, had managed to get me a message through military channels. It read, "Sister and husband killed in motorcycle accident.". I was *devastated.* My sister, Susie, and her husband, Carl, hadn't been married very long. I didn't know how they had been killed in a motorcycle accident,

though. I didn't even know that they owned a bike.
It didn't matter. All I knew was that they were
dead.

I was given special permission to try to call
home, but every number I called, I got no answer.
Mom and Dad were gone. Gay was gone. My in-
laws, Henry and Doris were gone. It seemed that
everyone was gone! Finally, I was able to reach my
Aunt Betty, and I asked her how Mom and Dad
were holding up, and if she knew where they were.
She said she thought that they were probably at the
funeral. When I told her about the message I had
received, and how it read, she gasped out loud
and said, "Oh my God! It wasn't Susie and Carl, it
was Sue and Ted - *Gay's* sister and her husband!". I
was *so* relieved that Susie and Carl were okay, but I
was still very upset about Sue and Ted. I decided to
wait a couple of hours before trying to reach Gay
again. When I finally reached her, she was a mess,
but she was still able to tell me what had happened.

Gay was living with her parents while I was
in Vietnam. At that time, they lived a half mile

north of Cheney, Kansas on the main road into town. Sue and Ted were married on May 1, 1971, at the Cheney Baptist Church. They had taken a short honeymoon and returned to Cheney. Ted was in the Navy, so they had loaded their car with their few belongings, and were preparing to leave the next day for Rhode Island - Ted's next duty station.

They borrowed Henry's little Honda 90, and rode into Cheney to say their good-byes to family and friends. They were returning to Henry and Doris' house at just about dusk, and when Ted slowed down to turn into the driveway, he and Sue were struck from behind at 70 M.P.H. - by a drunk driver. Gay had heard the crash, and came running out of the house. She was the first person to see the accident. I don't know how she was able to handle what she saw.

When I talked to her, I asked her if she wanted me to try to get emergency leave to come home and be with her. She thought about it for a bit, and finally said, "No. The funeral is over, and you being here won't change anything. Besides, you'll be coming home in a couple of months anyway. Let's just leave things the way they are." I knew then that I had married one tough lady.

About two weeks after their wedding, Sue and Ted's funeral was held at the same church where they were married. When they died, they were both twenty-one years old, and had been husband and wife for only ten days. I spent nearly two years in Vietnam, came home alive and healthy, and they died a half mile north of Cheney, Kansas. Somehow, it doesn't seem fair. I think I'll ask God about that when I see Him.

At Long Thanh, I shared a hooch with several other guys. Larry, Bob, Don, and "Francis" were pretty cool, but the real cut-up was John. I came into the hooch one day to find John sitting on his bunk, staring into space, and saying, "Gee!", over and over. When I asked him what he was doing, he grinned and said, "I've decided what I want to do when I get out of the Army. I want to be a "G-man". I'm practicing." That was almost too corny to laugh at, but we laughed anyway. John also had a habit of calling people a communist if they didn't agree with him about something - *anything.* For instance, if you told him that you really didn't care very much for apple pie, he was likely to say something like, "I suppose you don't like ice cream or baseball either, huh? What are you - *communist* or something?" Then, he would just grin. There was rarely a dull moment when John was around, and his sense of humor - however warped - helped keep our spirits up.

Some of my other friends really liked to smoke marijuana. I hadn't tried that stuff yet, and didn't intend to. However, my friends had other ideas about that. When I was about thirty days short, several of them got together and came over to the hooch with some grass. They told me that I had been too straight for too long, and they weren't going to leave until I smoked a joint with them. The way that they described this stuff made it sound too good to be true, and they were determined to get me to try it before I went home. Finally, and much to my shame, I gave in to the peer pressure. They showed me how to hold it, how to inhale it, and one of them even loaned me his roach clip so that I could finish it off. By the time I finished that joint, my mind was off somewhere in "La-La Land"!

I must explain here, that this was *not* your average, run-of-the-mill crabgrass like they were selling on the street corners in the States back then. This was what they called "Thai-stick". It was, and probably still is, very high in T.H.C. content, and would knock you on your can! It about knocked me on mine! The guys were laughing their heads off, seeing me high like that. The harder I tried to act sober, the more awkward I got, and that made them laugh even harder. They finally left, assured in their own minds that they had "done their duty". However, by that time, I was so messed up that I could hardly function. That grass *did* seem to be pretty good stuff, though. In fact, it was so good that it was *scary*!

I was brought up to believe that if something was "too good to be true", it usually was. Such was the case with the Thai-stick. I'm not a control freak, or anything like that, but I'm accustomed to being in control of my body and my mind. That night, I didn't have much control over either one. I finally made it over to my bunk and sat down, but something - in fact, *everything* seemed to still be moving. I put my elbows on my knees, my hands on either side of my head, and closed my eyes, but it didn't help. Something in my head was *still* moving, and I couldn't stop it!

I don't know how long I sat there like that, but some time during the night I must have laid down on the bunk, because that's where I was when I woke up the next morning. I had also overslept, but at that point, I really didn't care. I still didn't care when my platoon sergeant walked into the hooch, informed me that I had missed the morning formation, and asked me what was going on. I was still about two-thirds loopy, and I remember telling him that I had decided to sleep in. That was *not* the right thing to say! Sarge grabbed me by my t-shirt, pulled me to my feet, and looked me square in the eyes. Then he said, "Okay, I know what's goin' on with you now. 'Seen it lotsa times. Those damned pot-head buddies of yours got you high last night, didn't they? Well, they didn't do you any favors. You can get in big trouble messin' around with that junk!" That was when I got *really* stupid! I recall asking him, " So, how much trouble can I get in? What's the Army going to do - send me to Vietnam?"

His face turned beet red. I don't think I'd ever seen Sarge that mad before! Much to his credit, he let go of my t-shirt, took a step back, and just glared at me. I don't think he was counting to ten, either. Probably more like counting to a hundred! Finally, he said, "Look, Gower, you're a straight troop - always have been as far as I know. You've got a good record, and you'll be goin' back to the World in about a month, so don't start screwin' up *now!* You be down to the Nav. van in fifteen minutes, and I won't say anything to anybody." He turned to leave, and but stopped and added, "If you're *not* down there in fifteen minutes, rest assured that I will *personally* come back here and drag your sorry butt down to see the First Sergeant! Got me?" I told him that I understood.

That had to be the longest day that I ever spent in the Nav. van. I thought it would never end! As the day dragged on, I slowly started to sober up, and I started thinking about what Sarge had said to me that morning. It wasn't until much later that I truly realized what he had done for me that day. He had shaken me up, and brought me at least part way back to reality. It was then that I started remembering all of the guys that I had known through all of those months in 'Nam who had started smoking Thai-stick. Most of them stuck to the weed, but they got lazy, and didn't seem to care much about anything anymore - except for where and when they would get their next joint. Some of them graduated to the harder drugs and got really messed up.

Yes, there were reasons why I had steered clear of that stuff in the past, and I was remembering each and every one of them. It was then that I decided that one joint had nearly been one too many. No more! I swore off that junk, and have never been sorry for making that decision.

I pulled my final bunker guard duty in the last week of July, 1971. With my luck, I ended up spending the night in a bunker with a "newbee"(new guy in country). This kid had only been in Vietnam about a month, and he really didn't know much of anything about anything. Unlike Can Tho, our bunkers at Long Thanh North were two-man bunkers. The kid and I were assigned to bunker #31, which was down near the end of the runway. Bunker #31 was famous for its' smell. Every day, the pots under our latrines were collected, dumped at the end of the runway, and the contents was then set on fire with the help of a little jet fuel. The stench from those fires was nearly enough to gag a maggot, and the wind usually carried the smoke right over bunker #31. The good part about that was, the mosquitoes didn't like the smoke any more that we did, so we had to use very little, if any, of that nasty mosquito repellant.

We got everything set up in our bunker - our

M-16's, the M-60 machine gun, the M-79 grenade launcher, and the claymore mines - and then we exchanged small talk until sundown. That's when the kid pulled out a joint and lit it. I was immediately ticked off! I told him that guard duty was no place for that junk, and firmly "suggested" that he put it out. He didn't pay any attention to me, so I again told him to douse it, but he still ignored me. That was when I reached down and pressed the little lever on the side of my M-16 that released the bolt and slid a live round into the chamber. Since the weapon was laying across my lap, the barrel was pointing directly at his gut. Needless to say, I now had his undivided attention! He said, "Hey man, what are you doin'?! You're not really gonna shoot me over a joint, are ya?!" He looked at me for a while, and I could almost see the wheels turning in his head. He was really trying to think his way out of this situation. Finally, his face lit up like somebody had flipped a switch, and he said, "Oh, I get it! You want some too? Hey, no problem! I got plenty, man! You don't have to go getting radical on me!"

I just stared at him for a minute, since I couldn't hardly believe what I was hearing! How could anyone be *that* dense? I finally told him, "You just don't get it do ya, kid? I *asked* you to put that thing out. Then I *told* you to put it out. Are you gonna make me take the safety off this weapon too?"Now he was *really* getting nervous! "You really gonna kill me over a joint?!", he squealed. "No," I said, "I won't kill you, but I can sure make you wish that I had. What I'll do is blow one, or maybe both, of your kneecaps off. Then, every day for the rest of your life, when you wake up in the morning and look down at those stumps that you *used* to call legs, you will remember what that joint cost you. Now, PUT IT OUT!" He did.

"Man, you're crazy!", he said. I told him, "Look, kid, you just got here, and you've got a long time to go. You don't want to get messed up on that stuff - especially not on guard duty in a combat zone! If you're lucky, you won't get caught, but if you're not so lucky, you could either wind up dead, or the Army will throw you into L.B.J.(Long Binh Jail), and lose the key! As for me, I already know what that junk does to you, and I'm not gonna have you falling asleep or passing out on me tonight, so some V.C. sapper can slip through the wire and slit *both* of our throats! Crazy? Yeah, maybe I *am* a little crazy right now, but I've been in Vietnam a long time, and in a few days I plan to go back to the World alive and well - and maybe crazy, too. But if you and I are both dead, crazy won't matter much, will it? Do you *get* it now, kid?" We didn't talk much after that. It was a long night for both of us.

I actually had no intention of shooting the kid, but he didn't know that, so my bluff worked pretty well. Good thing he didn't push it, though. I put my brain into "think" mode for the rest of the night, and kept one eye on the perimeter, and the other eye on the kid. I don't remember the kid's name, or where he was from, but in retrospect, I really do hope that he made it back home all right.

When I was pulling guard duty at Can Tho, I would go into "think" mode, thinking about the present and the recent past, wondering if there was anything that I had done that I would have changed. At Long Thanh, I found myself thinking more about the future, and making plans for things that I wanted to accomplish in my lifetime. I thought about going back to college, to get that degree in architecture. I thought about maybe going to flight school, so that I might get a chance to apply for astronaut training. I even thought about what it was going to be like, setting up house with Gay, where we would live, where we would work, and all of that newlywed stuff. Strangely, of all the things that I thought about for all of those long hours on guard duty, the one thing that never even crossed my mind was someday writing a book. Funny how things turn out sometimes, isn't it?

By the time the first of August rolled around, I was too *short* to be seen with the naked eye. It wasn't going to be easy leaving my friends behind, but when it was my turn to do out-country processing, I was READY! This time, I was leaving Vietnam *for good!*

As my Freedom Bird sat on the taxi-way at Bien Hoa, I experienced all kinds of emotions. Mostly, I was excited and happy. I was also as nervous as "a long-tailed cat in a room full of rocking chairs", as my Dad says - hoping that nothing would go wrong. I was afraid, too.

There was no place on the planet that I would rather be at that time than *home,* but I was scared to be actually going there. I wasn't sure what kind of reception I would get - from the general public, I mean. Even though we were half-way around the world, we got the news on the radio, via the Armed Forces Vietnam Network. We knew what the mood was back home, concerning the war. We had heard reports about returning Vietnam vets who were "greeted" upon their return by insults, cursing, being spat upon, or having garbage (and worse) thrown at them. I was so happy, and yet so scared. God forbid that it should ever happen that way again.

Our aircraft *finally* taxied to the end of the runway, and waited for clearance to take off. I think there were about two hundred of us aboard - maybe more - and we had been waiting for this moment for a long time. The pilot set the brakes and gunned the engines. We were buckled in and ready to go. When the pilot released the brakes, the sudden acceleration set us all back in our seats. We picked up speed quickly as we rolled down the runway, and when we finally felt the wheels leave the ground, it got real quiet - for about ten or fifteen seconds, anyway. I guess we were just waiting, in case we came back down again. When we didn't – WOW! We nearly went berzerk! Jubilation wouldn't even come close to describing what we were feeling at that moment. It was far beyond that.

When we reached cruising altitude, we were able to unbuckle our seat belts and move around some. It had quieted down considerably, and the reality of what was happening to us was finally starting to sink in. It was going to be a long flight. It gave us a lot of time to think. We were on our way back to the *WORLD*, and though happier than happy, we were somewhat anxious, too. We wondered just how much the *world* had changed since we left. Or was it *we* who had changed? Probably both.

Gay and I had arranged to meet in California when I was released from active duty. We were going to spend a few days together in San Francisco before returning to Kansas. However, I was able to get on a flight that would leave twelve hours sooner than my original flight. Also, my new flight was going to the East coast, instead of California, and I would E.T.S.(Estimated Time of Separation - from active duty) at Fort Dix, New Jersey.

Our plane landed in Japan for fuel and servicing, and again in Alaska, before continuing on to the continental U.S.. I called Gay from Alaska, telling her of the change. We agreed that since it would take two or three days to process out of the Army, I would call her when I was released, give her my flight number, an we would meet in Dallas, Texas.

Her flight arrived in Dallas several hours before mine. Being a bit nervous, she called my uncle, Charlie Dundas, who lived in Dallas, and he picked her up at the airport. He took her back to his home, where he and Aunt Margaret comforted her and visited with her until time to return to the airport for my arrival. She told me later that they were wonderful to her, and she was glad that they were there to help her.

After being released from the Army, it took me a while to realize that, "Hey! I'm a *civilian* again!" I was still in uniform though, because I didn't have any civilian clothes with me. Gay was bringing my "civies" with her for our short stay in Dallas. Gay and Uncle Charlie met my flight, and when I saw her, I dropped everything that I was carrying and *ran* to her. I wrapped my arms around her, lifted her off the floor, swung her around, and kissed her smack on the mouth! That kiss lasted for a while!

Uncle Charlie was standing back a bit, and waited a little while before walking up to shake my hand and greet me. He was a very gentle and sensitive person, so I figure that he waited in order not to interrupt what he knew was a very special moment for Gay and me. Over the next couple for days, we visited with Uncle Charlie and Aunt Margaret, went to Six Flags Over Texas, and generally enjoyed being with each other again.

Finally, we said our good-byes and thanked Uncle Charlie and Aunt Margaret for being so kind to us. We boarded a plane for Wichita, Kansas, after calling home and letting the families know our arrival time. It wasn't a very long flight, so we just played cards with a deck of Texas Giant playing cards that we had bought just for fun.

Although I now had civies, I chose to wear my uniform home. I had left in uniform, and I would return in uniform. I wasn't sure what, if any, response that would evoke with the crowds at the airport (there were always anti-war protesters around in those days), but at this point, I was simply too happy to care.

After landing in Wichita, we taxied up to the terminal, where they rolled the steps out to the aircraft. After descending the steps, I paused for a moment to suck in that Kansas air! Then, I literally got down on my hands and knees and kissed the ground. Yes, I'm one of those people who actually did that, and was *glad* to have the opportunity. Over 58,000 of those who served in Vietnam never got that chance. I guess I was kissing the ground for them, too. It was okay now. My journey was over. This was Kansas. This was home.

CHAPTER NINE

FITTING IN

I don't expect today's generation to understand what the mood in our country was like when I returned from Vietnam in August of 1971. You would have had to have been there at that time to be able to comprehend it fully, but I will try my best to describe how it was.

Patriotism was at an all-time low - almost nonexistent. The stars and stripes were just "the flag". The Nation Anthem was just something that was *endured* as a ritual performed prior to some sporting event. "God Bless America", and "America The Beautiful" were rarely, if ever, heard. Suffice it to say that they were not among the songs that were on America's "Top Ten" list. There were no yellow ribbons, no parades or marching bands welcoming the troops home. No "fly-overs".

Nothing. Except for the news, the subject of Vietnam was strictly *taboo*. Few people, if any, cared to bring up the subject - especially in public. It just wasn't done.

There was also a stigma attached to the returning veterans. I believe that it was someone in the media who coined a phrase that I *hate* to this day. We were referred to as "drug-crazed baby killers". It was no wonder then, that we were perceived by the general public as "weird", or "strange", or "psychos". It was thought by many that any or all of us could go ballistic at the drop of a hat! I don't deny that many Vietnam vets had problems after the war. Some of them may have suffered because of the drugs that they were introduced to over there. Drugs of all kinds were both plentiful and accessible, but that doesn't mean that we all became hooked the minute we set foot in Vietnam. Most of those having mental problems, I believe, were suffering due to a combination of the horrors of war, and the rejection - and sometimes abuse - that they encountered upon their return.

I would get a wary look from someone once in a while, but I didn't let it bother me. I knew that I didn't fit into any of the categories that people were trying to put me in, so I figured that it was *their* problem.

Was I crazy? No. A teeny bit *nuts*? Maybe. But then, I don't ever remember being accused of being "normal" *before* I went to 'Nam. So, who's to decide? I think that we can *all* get a little bit nuts once in a while. It's human nature, but it doesn't mean that we're *freaks*.

With so many returning from Vietnam, and in such numbers, jobs weren't exactly plentiful when I got back. My father-in-law, Henry Stoll, offered to let me work for him. He was a homebuilder then, and a finish carpenter by trade. He taught me homebuilding for the ground up - literally. I learned a lot from Henry, and from my mother-in-law, Doris, too. She worked beside Henry, doing sanding, staining, varnishing, and ceramic tile work. Gay and I settled in Cheney, Kansas, where she was raised, and where Henry,

Doris, and I were building houses. Gay was - and still is - a beautician.

By the time our first daughter, Kim, was born, it was March of 1973. I was feeling a need for change. I applied at Cessna Aircraft Company in Wichita, and was hired as a final assembly electrician - a job which I owe to my avionics training in the Army. I worked there for four months, and got laid off along with many others. I really liked that job.

After Cessna, I spent the next nineteen years working for the Sedgwick County Rural Electric Cooperative - twelve years as a lineman on the line crew, and the last seven years as Staking Engineer. The business was based in Cheney, so we didn't have to relocate, although we moved several times in the area. During that time, our son Tim was born, in 1975, followed two years later by our youngest daughter, Melanie. Kim, Tim, and Melanie are grown now, with families of their own, and have blessed Gay and I with eight really *terrific* grandkids.

Through the years, we had our ups and downs, lean times and good times - just like all of the "normal" people that we knew. I thought that Vietnam would eventually become only a distant memory, but it was not to be.

Sometime in the Spring of 1978, I was contacted by my old alma mater, Maize High School. It seems that the students were coming up on the chapter in the history books that covered the Vietnam War, and they asked me if I would mind sitting in on a class, to perhaps make a comment or two about my involvement in the war, from a personal point of view. History books?! I hadn't even *thought* about the Vietnam War being in the history books already! Anyway, since I had graduated from Maize High with the class of 1967, I felt that, as an alumnus, I couldn't very easily turn down their request. Besides, if these young people could benefit in any way from my experience, I felt that I owed it to the next generation to let them know how I felt about the situation. I agreed to the proposal, and a date and time were set.

After I agreed to do this History class thing, I started to get a little nervous about it. People still didn't talk about Vietnam, even then. Also, I wondered how I should dress for this upcoming occasion. Jungle boots? Fatigue shirt and jeans? Dress green uniform? I finally decided against "all of the above". With the stigma still attached to Vietnam veterans, I figured that they might expect that kind of stuff. So, when the day arrived for my visit, I put on my three-piece suit, and went to Maize High.

As it turned out, it wasn't just *a* History class. Several classes had been combined, and they had allotted *two hours* for my visit. I was introduced to the students, and then began telling my story - pretty much like it is related in this book. I told them right up front that I couldn't speak for all of the Vietnam vets - only for myself. I also told them that I was no war hero, and if they were expecting to hear stories of bloody combat, and "pot"parties, they were going to be greatly disappointed. I was not going to lie to them about anything, nor was I going to make up stories just to make this class more interesting.

After I had briefly related my story, I opened up the class for questions and answers - telling the students that I would answer *all* questions put to me, to the best of my ability. These young people were born much closer to the actual event than the students of today, and they were genuinely curious, since nobody was talking about the war. They had really good, honest questions about a variety of things.

Everything was going smoothly, until one rather uncouth youth asked THE question - the one that you're not supposed to ask. What bothered me the most, was the way in which he asked it. He raised his hand, and when I pointed to him, he asked, "So, how many people did *you* blow away, man?" It got really quiet in that room - for about ten seconds. Some of the students were just staring at this kid, with their mouths wide open. Others were looking at *me*, I guess to see how I was reacting to the question. Suddenly, a number of these young people began loudly berating this kid for asking such a question. One young man stood up, addressing the "offender", and said, "Are you *nuts*?! You don't ask somebody about a thing like that!" When it looked as though the situation might get out of hand, I raised my hands and asked for quiet. I then asked them to all please be seated, and reminded them that I had agreed to answer *all* questions. I then informed them that I would answer this one, too.

I began by addressing the young man who had asked the question. I told him, "You're friend was right. This is *not* a question that you want to ask a Vietnam veteran, or a veteran of any other war, for that matter. There are people who have spent a long time trying to forget what they saw and what they had to do during wartime, and they don't care to be reminded of those things. The way that you asked the question was both rude and crude. If you *ever* decide to ask that question of someone again, I hope that you will show a little bit of "class", and be more sensitive about the way that you phrase it."

"I will tell you this - I was rated Expert with every weapon on which I was tested, including the M-16 rifle, which was standard issue in Vietnam. I was accustomed to hitting whatever was in my sights. However, most weapons training is done in daylight, and the only time that I ever had to fire my weapon to defend myself, it was in the dark."

"One night when I was on bunker guard at Can Tho, some *idiot* - don't know which side he was on - popped off a round or two, and a short fire-fight ensued. I say that it was short, because the bunkers on our whole side of the perimeter opened up on the enemy location. Not only that, but when the Cobra gunship that we always had circling the airfield saw where the enemy fire was coming from, he made a pass with his mini-guns and "took care of business". The whole incident was over very quickly".

"In explanation, a mini-gun is quite simply, a high-tech electric Gattling gun. It fires so many rounds, so fast, that it cannot be fired at full tilt but for a short time. Otherwise, the barrels will start to melt. Every sixth round in the ammo chain is a "tracer" round. When fired, it leaves a red trail behind it, so that you can see where you're firing in the dark."

"The firing from the Cobra that night looked like a red laser beam, and sounded like a chainsaw. That's pretty awesome firepower, when you consider that you're only seeing every sixth round. A human being can't run fast enough or duck down low enough to escape something like that. That's why the fire-fight ended so quickly. In the morning, enemy bodies were recovered."

"Finally, in answer to your question - did one of my bullets actually take someone's life? I don't know - and I don't want to know. That's how I handle *that*."

As a result of my visit to Maize High School, I began visiting other schools in the area. During the next three or four years, I regularly allotted one week of my vacation per year to visit these schools. I spoke to hundreds of students, and never had a negative response, as I recall.

During the years that I gave those classes, I was asked one particular question many times, and it's a question for which I really had no answer. The question was this: "What's it going to take for America to finally "get over" the Vietnam war ?" Now *that's* a tough one! After all, being a Vietnam Veteran doesn't make me an expert on the entire war, or the problems that were and are a result of it.

I've spent many, many hours trying to find the answer to that question. In part, because I've had to leave the students with an empty cup by simply saying, "I really just don't know. I don't know if anyone in this country can now or ever will be able to answer that question to everyone's satisfaction. I'm sorry, but I don't have an answer right now, either."

I know it's a question that needs to be answered, but I think it's also a question that I and many other Americans have been avoiding for a long time. I guess I never really pursued the answer as diligently as I should, because I was afraid that if

I did find it, I would get frustrated to the point of going off the deep end, if nobody else discovered it too.

However, after much thought, I think that I may have at least a *partial* answer. It may not be *the* answer that we've all been looking for, and it may not be a cure for the "Vietnam Virus", but I think that it would at least be a start - or *would have been.* Unfortunately, in order to have the most effect, this answer would have had to have been implemented many years ago. It probably wouldn't work today. Are you ready for this?

How about an apology? - a *national* apology. I know how ridiculous that must sound, and I fully understand how drastic a step that would be. However, perhaps something drastic is what is needed, and it's not like the Vietnam vets don't deserve it - they do. It wouldn't have to be anything eloquent or elaborate. Something simple, like, "We're sorry that we sent you fine people half-way around the world to do a job, and then called you home before the job was done. We're sorry that we put you in harm's way for so long, while we were trying to make up our minds how best to pursue the war. We're sorry that some of us chose to treat you like second-class citizens after your return from Vietnam. You did all that was asked of you - and more - and there is no shame in that, regardless of the outcome."

Who would make this apology? The President? Doubtful. Some other high-ranking government official? Not likely, unless he or she were trying to make points during an election year. This apology would have to be *sincere*, and unfortunately, sincerity is just as hard to find among our elected representatives now, as it was during the Vietnam war. No, I think this apology should begin at the grass-roots level. However, I won't hold my breath waiting for an apology, however it might come about, and it would be too little - too late, anyway.

Okay, if an apology isn't the answer, then what is? How about a simple "Thank You"? It's hardly ever too late to say, "Thanks!" Whether it comes from a lofty politician, or down-home folks, a simple *thank you* will always be appreciated. Something like, "Thank you for serving your country in a time of need, instead of running off to a foreign country to avoid the draft. Thank you for your efforts while serving in Vietnam, and the hardships you endured and the sacrifices you made on behalf of your country. And thank you for the contributions you have made to America since your return from Vietnam." That's plain, simple, and not difficult to do. In fact, it can be done on a *personal* level quite easily.

When visiting with all of those history students, I encouraged them to try something a little out of the ordinary. I told them, "If you personally know someone who served in South Vietnam, whether a relative, friend, or an acquaintance, ask yourself a few short questions. For instance, " Do I really like this person? Has his or her life made a difference in *my* life? Can I honestly and sincerely say that I am thankful that this person made it back from Vietnam? If the answer to any one of these questions is "yes", do yourself, your country, and - most importantly- that Vietnam veteran a *big* favor: TELL HIM."

Looking back, I think that I *did* give those young people at least a partial answer to their "unanswerable" question, although I was quite unaware of it at the time. Also, I really have no way of knowing what effect, if any, my little challenge may have had on those students, or the Vietnam veterans with whom they were acquainted.

I finally quit giving the classes, because for some reason that I cannot yet explain, it got more and more difficult to tell the story. I'm sure some psychiatrist would have a field day with that scenario.

Anyway, I felt as though I had made at least a small contribution to the further education of those young people, so I didn't feel too badly about quitting, if they had benefited somewhat. I guess that writing this book is like giving my last class. I'm O.K. with that.

CHAPTER TEN

P. T. S. D.

Post-Traumatic Stress Disorder is what they call it, I think. I was more fortunate than most. It affected me only once, and it only lasted a few hours. It is not an experience that I would care to repeat - mainly because of the extreme depression, and the feeling of helplessness that goes with it.

I remember in November of 1979, when Iranian "students" stormed the American Embassy in Tehran, and took the embassy personnel hostage. I was still working at the Rural Electric at the time. Gay and I, and our three small children were living in a small rented farmhouse about three miles east of Cheney. I think that was about the time that ABC News started their *Nightline* program. Gay and I would watch that show every night, to find out the progress of the negotiations for the release of the hostages. Those people were held captive for 444 days.

Finally, shortly after Ronald Reagan was sworn in as President of the United States, the hostages were released. During their captivity, yellow ribbons were tied to trees, porch posts, utility poles, vehicle radio antennas, and fence posts - to be taken down only when our people were returned. We thought that was a neat thing to do, and we cried tears of joy when we watched the celebrations and honors that were bestowed upon those people. It seemed that patriotism had been revived! The celebrations were elaborate, and went on for some time. We were happy for those people, too. They had endured a *lot*, and they deserved that kind of welcome.

There were parades, with American flags and yellow ribbons flying everywhere, "fly-overs", speeches - the whole ball of wax. It was GREAT! One evening, after we had put the kids to bed, Gay and I were watching one of those celebrations, when she began to sob. When I asked her what was the matter, she put her arms around me and said, "I wish you had gotten that kind of welcome. You deserve it too." I guess that's when it finally struck me. She was right. As I explained earlier, I knew that there would be none of this type of celebration when I returned from Vietnam, and since I didn't expect it, I guess I never really missed it. That's why it never bothered me - until that night.

I got up off the couch and put on my coat. I told Gay that I was going outside for a smoke. She told me much later that she knew something was wrong then, because I *never* went outside to smoke - especially not in winter.

I walked out to our garden spot, which was in a large clearing East of the farmhouse. I lit a cigarette and looked up at the night sky. It was so clear that night, that I swear you could see every star in the heavens with the naked eye. There was no wind - unusual for Kansas. It was dead calm, and very quiet. It didn't seem particularly cold, either - also unusual for a Kansas winter. I had stood some old cinder blocks on end at the edge of the garden, so I sat down on one and just gazed up into the night sky for what seemed to be a very long time. That's when the tears started to come.

You must understand that at this point in my life, I was not yet a Christian. I never stopped Gay from taking the kids to Sunday school or church, but at that time I didn't really feel the need to be there myself. I believed that there was a God, but I wasn't sure exactly who He was, or where I stood with Him. I wasn't much of a praying-type person then, but I talked to God that night. I was angry. I was disappointed. I was hurt. It all seemed so very, very unfair.

I looked up into the heavens and started talking to God - out loud. I asked Him, "God, if you're up there listening, I need to know something. What did I ever do *not* to deserve the kind of welcome home that those brave hostages got? What did any of us Vietnam vets do *not* to deserve that kind of welcome home from our country? Didn't we come when we were called? Didn't we go where we were sent? Didn't we do our best to serve our country with honor? It's not fair! It's just *not fair!*"

By this time, I was crying like a newborn baby. I cried until there were no tears left, then I just sat there with my head down on my knees. I guess I was waiting for an answer from God. Of course, God didn't speak back to me - He never has. I think that He heard me, though. God is a very good listener. I think He gave me an answer in the form of a memory of something someone had said to me several years earlier, during the short time that I had worked at Cessna. Those words kept coming into my head, over and over.

I had been then, and still am, a student of the philosophy that "could'a, would'a, should'a" can't change anything. What's done is done, and pity-parties don't accomplish anything positive. Finally, I realized that the welcome home that I *thought* I had missed, had already happened several years earlier. It was all that I would get, and ultimately, all that I would ever need. Those words kept running through my mind. God had given me an answer. It was okay now. The pity-party was over.

CHAPTER ELEVEN

GLAD YOU'RE BACK!

As previously mentioned, I went to work for Cessna Aircraft in July, 1973, as a final assembly electrician. I was on second shift, which didn't set too well with Gay, since I didn't get home until after midnight. She and our infant daughter, Kimberly, were home by themselves in the evenings. I was also working four hours a day for Henry, too, so I just slept when I could. We had bills piled up, and this was the only way that I could think of to pay them down. Gay and Kimmy were asleep when I got home from Cessna. When I got up to go to work for Henry, Kimmy wanted to play, but I had to leave. When I came home to get ready to go to work at Cessna, Kimmy was down for a nap. It was depressing, hardly ever seeing Gay and Kimmy, but we had a good time on the weekends, and the bills were getting paid.

Since I was wiring inside the aircraft - tailcones, to be exact - one of the safety requirements was that I had to wear leather boots, or high-top leather shoes. I couldn't afford to buy new shoes, so I wore my old leather combat boots that I had worn in Basic and Signal School.

Summers in Kansas are *hot*, even on the night shift. Combine that with working in a huge aircraft factory(not air-conditioned), and then working inside the tailcone of a new aircraft, and you can generate some serious sweat! My feet were burning up in those leather boots, and I could hardly wait to get them off when I got home each night. The smell was horrific, too! It finally dawned on me that I still had a pair of jungle boots left over from 'Nam. They had a tough sole, and the toes and heels were leather. The rest was a composite material that allowed the feet to "breathe". I checked with my supervisor, Carl, and he said that it would be all right to wear them instead of the all-leather combat boots that I had been wearing.

GLAD YOU'RE BACK!

The electrician's bay was at the rear of the final assembly line. Across the aisle from us was the upholstery department. At lunch time and during breaks, those of us in final assembly would line up along our side of the aisle to eat, drink a can of soda, grab a quick smoke, or just visit with each other. The ladies from the upholstery department did much the same on their side of the aisle. We usually didn't converse much with them, and vice-versa.

Shortly after I began wearing the jungle boots to work, I was eating lunch and just looking around - minding my own business - when I noticed that one of the ladies across the aisle kept glancing in my direction, looking down at my feet. I knew that even with the jungle boots on, my feet were still pretty rank, but I was hoping that the smell wasn't bothering people *that* far away! I finally realized that it wasn't so much my feet that she kept looking at, but my *boots*. Oh, well, no big deal. For all she knew, I could've bought those boots at a local Army/Navy store.

This went on for several days. During that time, I took notice of her footwear, too - moccasins. I also noticed that she had very dark hair, big brown eyes, a beautiful wedding ring, and a great smile - lots of perfectly white teeth. And she was short. Very short.

One evening during lunch, I glanced in her direction, and she was once again looking at my boots. Then she looked up at me. Our eyes met for only a spit second before she quickly turned her head away - embarrassed, I guess. When the horn blew, signaling the end of our lunch period, I stood and began putting my lunch stuff away. When I had finished, I turned around and there she was - standing right in front of me. She pointed down at my feet and said, "Those are jungle boots, aren't they?" I was a bit taken aback, so I could only reply, "Yes Ma'am, they are." Then she looked up at me with a very serious, but questioning look on her face, and asked, " How long were you there?" I was shocked! She knew. She didn't even mention Vietnam. She didn't have to. She just *knew.* I was stunned to the point of near speechlessness. Knowing that most people didn't talk about 'Nam back then, I kept my answer brief by simply replying, " Well, long enough."

She then did something that I treasure even to this day. She looked up at me and smiled - great big - and said, "Glad you're back!" She then turned and quickly walked away. I was again shocked, and yet elated almost to tears. *Tears of joy.*

Here was a woman who didn't know me from Adam. Having recognized my jungle boots for what they were, she somehow knew that I had been to Vietnam, and felt compelled to give me a very personal welcome home. What a marvelous gift! I know that she was speaking for herself, but to me it was much, much more than that. It was as though she was speaking for all of those millions of Americans who felt the same way she did, but who had never expressed it. To me, she was speaking for my country, but in a very personal way.

I don't know how she knew about the boots. Maybe she had a brother, a cousin, an uncle, or a friend who had served in Vietnam. Maybe even her husband. Maybe she had lost someone close to her in that war. However she knew, it didn't matter to me. She had given me a gift that was worth more than all of the parades, marching bands, speeches, awards and other accolades put together. It's all that I needed - and more.

Those three small words were what kept running through my mind that night out in the garden, years later. They are probably what has helped me keep my sanity, and at least a semblance of normalcy in my life all these years since the war in Vietnam.

I did manage to mumble a few words of thanks to this kind lady during the next break, all the while fighting back the tears. I am ashamed to say that I never formally introduced myself to her, or even spoke to her after that. I still don't know her name. I was laid off - with many others - shortly after this incident. I never saw her again after Cessna,but those three words, "Glad you're back!", will remain in my heart *forever.*

GLAD YOU'RE BACK!

GOD BLESS AMERICA

ACKNOWLEDGEMENTS

I wish to thank my daughters, Kim and Melanie, for their help in preparing this manuscript. Their loving words of encouragement and expertise on the computer have helped me put my thoughts into words and my words into legible script – at least, that is my hope.

I also wish to thank Mrs. Shirley Dyck, who taught me English Literature at Maize High School, and instilled in me an appreciation for the literary arts. She has not only been a fine teacher, but a friend, as well.

I cannot thank Mr. Ernest L. Smith enough. He was my English Comp. and Creative Writing teacher at Maize High School. His dedication to his profession and high standards have allowed me to put my thoughts onto paper, hopefully in a way that will be clearly understood by all who read them.

I also appreciate the example of my Maize High School football, basketball, and track coach, Mr. Augustine Ledesma. He always promoted the philosophy that if you want to do something, plan to give it a 100% effort from the beginning, or don't even bother to start. Well, I started this project, and now I've finished. Thank you, "Coach"!

Also, many, many thanks to my friend, David Rich. *I owe you!*